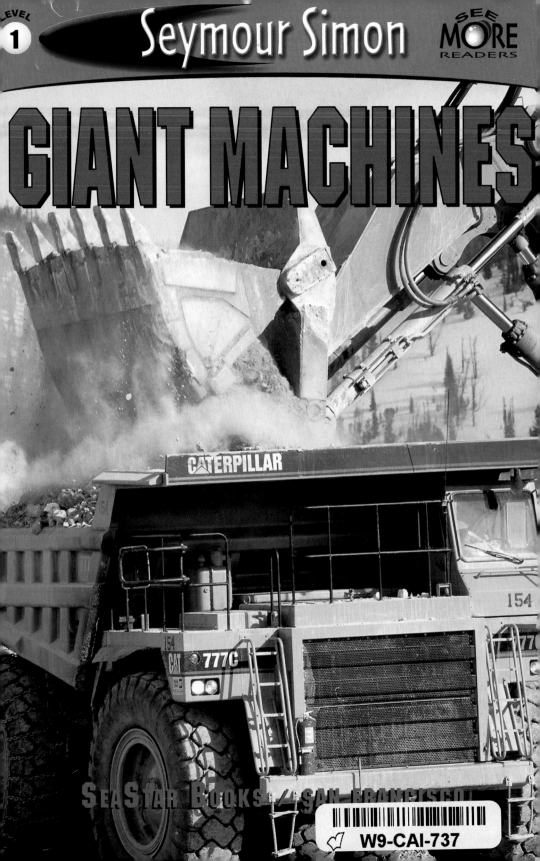

LEVEL 1

Seymour Simon

SEE MORE READERS

GIANT MACHINES

CATERPILLAR

154

CAT 777C

154

777

SeaStar Books / San Francisco

W9-CAI-737

To David Reuther,
with many thanks for his vision about this series.

Special thanks to reading consultant Dr. Linda B. Gambrell, Director of the School of Education at Clemson University, past president of the National Reading Conference, and past board member of the International Reading Association.

Permission to use the following photographs is gratefully acknowledged:
front cover, title page: © Dan Lamont/Corbis; pages 2–3, 30–31: © John Eastcott/YVA Momatiuk, Photo Researchers, Inc.; pages 4–5: © David Seawell/First Light; pages 6–7: © Komatsu Mining Systems; pages 8–9, 24–25: © Camerique/H. Armstrong Roberts; pages 10–11, 18–19: © W. Metzen/H. Armstrong Roberts; pages 12–13: Richard Hamilton Smith/Corbis; pages 14–15: © Paul Chesley/Tony Stone Images; pages 16–17: © Smith/Zefia/H. Armstrong Roberts; pages 20–21: © G. Ryan & S. Beyer/Tony Stone Images; pages 22–23: © Keith Wood/Tony Stone Images; pages 26–27: © M. Gibson/H. Armstrong Roberts; pages 28–29: © Mitch Kezar/Tony Stone Images; page 32: © Stephen Homer/First Light.

Text © 2002 by Seymour Simon.
All rights reserved.

Manufactured in China.

SeaStar is an imprint of Chronicle Books LLC.

Library of Congress Cataloging-in-Publication Data is available.

ISBN 1-58717-127-9

Distributed in Canada by Raincoast Books
9050 Shaughnessy Street, Vancouver, British Columbia V6P 6E5

10 9 8 7 6 5 4 3 2

Chronicle Books LLC
85 Second Street, San Francisco, California 94105

www.chroniclekids.com

Giant machines help us do work.

This giant shovel
can move a mountain.
A giant earthmover
can carry a load that weighs
as much as 50 elephants.

This bulldozer blade
is as big as a billboard.
It can tear huge rocks
out of the ground,
or it can push trees aside.
One blade scoops up enough
dirt to fill a dump truck.

A scraper is like a shovel and
a wheelbarrow working together.
Scrapers cut up the ground
and carry the dirt away.

A front-end loader
lifts and moves dirt.
A giant loader can carry
a weight equal to that of
a big school bus.

This giant dump truck
is as tall and as wide
as a two-story house.
Its engine weighs
as much as four
pickup trucks.

Its tires are twice as tall as a person.

This dragline is a giant crane with a digging bucket at the end.

In 50 days, a person
with a shovel can dig
a big hole.
A dragline can dig that hole
in one minute.

Bucket wheel excavators
scoop up huge amounts
of coal or dirt.
The largest excavators are
more than 600 feet long
and weigh nearly
30 million pounds.

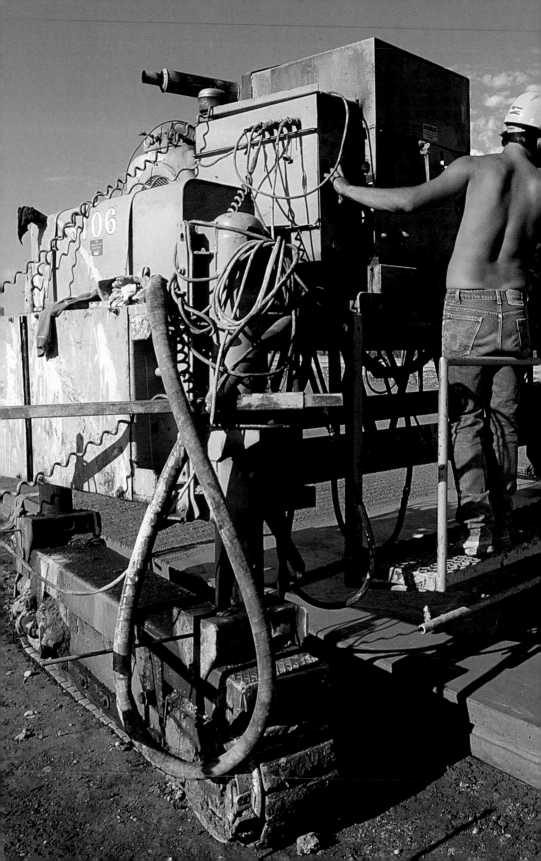

Pavers lay hot asphalt or
wet concrete onto the ground.

Then they flatten and smooth
it to make roads for cars
or runways for airplanes.

Tower cranes lift heavy loads

on skyscrapers, bridges,

shipyards, and mines.

These tower cranes

are 300 feet high,

the length of

a football field.

This offshore oil rig stands as tall as a skyscraper. It sits on legs that go 1,000 feet below the surface of the ocean. Giant cranes and drills pump thousands of barrels of oil a day.

This giant crawler carries a space shuttle to the launchpad at the Kennedy Space Center. The crawler travels at only one mile per hour. You can walk faster than that. But the crawler carries an 11–million–pound load.

A tub grinder
crushes boards
and wood waste.
Inside the tub,
huge steel wheels
smash the wood.
The chips
can be used
for fuel or mulch.

This 15-foot tub grinder
fills four big dump trucks
in one hour.

Farmers

use tractors

to pull machines

that help them

grow and harvest

their crops.

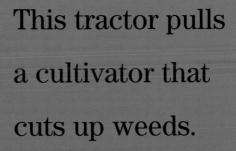

This tractor pulls a cultivator that cuts up weeds.

A combine cuts wheat,
corn, or bean plants.
In seconds, it separates
the crop from the stalks
and spits the grain or seeds
into a nearby truck.

A combine can harvest

100 acres of wheat a day.

Giant machines cut, carry,

and move all kinds of things

from one place to another.

Next time you see a big machine,

can you guess what it does?

If you liked learning about **Giant Machines**, you will also enjoy

LEVEL 1

Big Bugs
Killer Whales
Planets Around the Sun
Wild Bears

LEVEL 2

Danger! Earthquakes
Skyscrapers
Super Storms

LEVEL 3

Danger! Earthquakes
Pyramids & Mummies
Space Travelers

SEYMOUR SIMON is a former teacher and the author of more than 200 science books for children, more than half of which have been named Outstanding Science Trade Books for Children by the National Science Teachers Association. In addition to his series about the human body, space, and natural phenomena, Mr. Simon has written numerous books about earth's most compelling creatures, including *Whales, Gorillas, Sharks, Wolves,* and *Crocodiles and Alligators.* He is also the author of *Animals Nobody Loves* and *Out of Sight: Pictures of Hidden Worlds.*

Mr. Simon is the recipient of many awards honoring the body of his work, among them the *Washington Post*/Children's Book Guild Award; the Hope S. Dean Memorial Award, presented by the Boston Public Library; and the Knickerbocker Award for Juvenile Literature, presented by the New York Public Library Association.

Mr. Simon lives in Great Neck, New York. To see more, visit his web site at www.seymoursimon.com.

Front cover photograph © Dan Lamont/Corbis
Back cover photograph © Stephen Homer/First Light
Designed by Matthew Siee

**Earthmovers move mountains.
Crawlers carry space shuttles.
Can you guess what a
tower crane can lift?**

Dig into

GIANT MACHINES

and *SeeMore!*

Fritz's Classroom Library
Bin # JSB